Little Red Hen is Cooking

Based on a folk tale
by Rob Arego

NATIONAL
GEOGRAPHIC
LEARNING

Little Red Hen is cooking.
'What are you cooking?' asks Cat.

'Help me cook the soup,' says Hen.
'No,' says Cat.

4

'What are you cooking?' asks Cat.

'Biscuits,' says Hen. 'Do you like biscuits?'
'Yes, I do!' says Cat.

'Help me make the biscuits,' says Hen. 'No,' says Cat.

'What are you eating and drinking?' Cat asks.

'May I have soup and biscuits, please?' asks Cat.

Facts About Food

Eggs come from chickens.

Milk comes from cows.

Oranges come from trees.

Mmm! Tasty!

Bananas come from trees, too.

13

Fun with Food

Do you eat it or drink it?

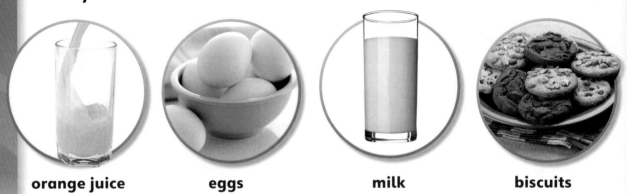

orange juice   eggs   milk   biscuits

Eat	Drink
eggs	

Look at the letters. Write the food word.

nabnaa

banana

geg

_____

upos

_____

lkmi

_____

Glossary

cat

help

hen / chicken